CONQUEROR

SET IN SOUL

© 2018 Tatiana Media LLC in partnership with Set In Soul LLC

ISBN #: 978-1-949874-99-0

Published by Tatiana Media LLC

All rights reserved. No part of this journal/publication may be reproduced, stored in a retrieval system, or transmitted in any form or by any means, electronic, mechanical, photocopying, recording, scanning, or otherwise, except as permitted under Section 107 or 108 of the 1976 United States Copyright Act whatsoever without express written permission from the author, except in the case of brief quotations embodied in critical articles and reviews. Please refer all pertinent questions to the publisher.

Limit of Liability/Disclaimer of Warranty: While the publisher and author have used their best efforts in preparing this book/journal, they make no representations or warranties with respect to the accuracy or completeness of the contents of this book/journal and specifically disclaim any implied warranties. The advice and strategies contained herein may not be suitable for your situation. You should consult with a professional where appropriate. Neither the publisher nor author shall be liable for any loss of profit or any other emotional, physical, spiritual and mental distress and damages, including but not limited to special, incidental, consequential, or other damages.

For general information on our other products and services, please contact our Customer Support within the United States at support@setinsoul.com.

Tatiana Media LLC as well as Set In Soul LLC publishes its books in a variety of electronic formats. Some content that appears in print may not be available in electronic books.

THIS JOURNAL BELONGS TO

_____

DEDICATED TO THE HEARTS
THAT JUST GOT STRONGER.
THE BIGGER THE HEART,
THE BIGGER THE VICTORY.

TABLE OF CONTENTS

How To Use This Journal	6
About Me	7
Mind Reset	9
The Conqueror Blueprint	31

HOW TO USE THIS JOURNAL

Your doctor told you that you have breast cancer. Everything your doctor said after that you tuned out because you were shocked after you heard your diagnosis. It's been weeks, and now you are experiencing anger or denial or maybe even depression. Each day it gets tougher to live your best life when you have thoughts that tell you to give up because the outcome to your diagnosis may be unfavorable. We know that those thoughts are all lies. Just like any challenge, this one is no different. You can overcome this challenge. In fact, you were built for this. You may be thinking why you and why at your age? But guess what. None of that matters. It's time for a new life. You can have that new life by making changes to your lifestyle and mentally expecting better. Obstacles don't stop because you think you're doing well in life or things are already challenging. Noooooooo. Obstacles come to strengthen you and show you who God is in every situation. It's time to summon up strength, courage, and the faith you never knew you had. Your new life needs these traits, and you are about to get through this as a fighter. Be willing to fight for yourself. When you fight for you, you are also fighting for others who need to see what it takes to become a conqueror.

This journal was created to remove any negative mindset about your current journey with breast cancer. With this journal, you will be able to keep track of your healing and show up each day with the determination to make today better than the day before. This is an honest place. Whether good or bad, you can jot down your thoughts and feelings here with no judgment. You are not allowed to feel bad for feeling bad. You can laugh, smile, and grow in strength and wisdom knowing better. We recommend that you fill out the daily prompt pages every night before going to bed. Reflect on your day and decide how the next day will be. There are motivational quotes sprinkled throughout this journal so you can fall in love with the conqueror you are. There are also daily affirmations to repeat to yourself to improve the way you talk to yourself and the way you address cancer. You will find freestyling pages spread throughout this journal so you can write down whatever comes to mind. You must know that this isn't the end but a new beginning. You are a conqueror. If no one has told you … we're proud of you for all you're fighting and pushing through that no one knows about. Let's get started.

ABOUT ME

ABOUT ME

I Am (Write Your Current Age):_____

My Doctor Is:_____

My Surgical Oncologist Is:_____

I Was Diagnosed On (Write The Date):_____

What Stage Am I In?_____

I Am Currently Getting Treated By:_____

Is This My First Time With Breast Cancer?_____

MIND RESET

MIND RESET

What I Didn't Know About Breast Cancer:

Does Anyone In My Family Currently Have Breast Cancer?

Has Anyone In My Family Ever Been Diagnosed With Breast Cancer?

Do I Know Any Breast Cancer Survivors?

I Currently Have To Go Through:

MIND RESET

How Did I Find Out I Have Breast Cancer?

My Support System Currently Consist Of:

The Moment My Doctor Told Me My Diagnoses, I Felt:

I Cry Over:

I Dream About:

MIND RESET

I Am Scared:

I Believe That The Reason Why I Have Breast Cancer:

I Am Angry That:

It's Important For Me:

What I Love About My Breast:

MIND RESET

What I Love About My Body:

Some Days I Feel:

It Hurts Me To Think:

When I Feel Down, I Pick Myself Up By:

I Never Thought:

MIND RESET

I Know I Am Strong Enough:

The First Person That I Told That I Was Diagnosed With Breast Cancer (Answer If Applicable):

The First Person That I Told That I Was Diagnosed With Breast Cancer Reacted (Answer If Applicable):

When I Told My Family I Was Diagnosed With Breast Cancer (Answer If Applicable):

When I Told My Friends I Was Diagnosed With Breast Cancer (Answer If Applicable):

MIND RESET

The Reason Why Some People Still Don't Know I Have Been Diagnosed With Breast Cancer (Answer If Applicable):

I Didn't Expect:

I Expected:

Once I Conquer This, I Will:

I Spend My Time:

MIND RESET

I Focus On:

What's Important To Me Right Now?

It's Hard For Me:

What's Been Helping Me To Keep Everything Together?

I Now Look At Life:

MIND RESET

I Am Now Choosing To Live My Life:

I Remember:

As A Woman With Breast Cancer (Answer If This Applies To You):

As A Man With Breast Cancer (Answer If This Applies To You):

I Feel Like Other People:

MIND RESET

What I've Felt Like I've Lost:

What I've Felt Like I've Gained:

I Feel Like I Am Handling My Diagnoses:

The Emotions I Have Felt So Far:

I Have Done My Best To:

MIND RESET

I Get Tired:

Financially, I Am:

I Wish Others Understood:

I Am Glad That:

Because Of Breast Cancer, I Am Forced To Change:

MIND RESET

Going Through This Challenging Season, I Have Learned:

I Believe:

I Know:

I Have Lived Through:

I Am Happy That:

MIND RESET

I Have Hope:

There Is A Misconception That:

I No Longer Worry:

I Now Do More:

I Now Do Less:

MIND RESET

I Stopped Doing:

I Am Proving:

When People See Me, I Want Them To See:

I Want God To:

I Thank God For:

MIND RESET

This Will Not Stop Me From:

I Gain Strength From:

Truthfully, I Just Want:

I Feel Like I Was Living (Before The Diagnoses):

I Feel Like I Am Living (After The Diagnoses):

MIND RESET

I Start My Days:

I End My Days:

When It's Time For Treatment, I Go In:

When It's Time For Treatment, I Feel:

When I See The Doctor, I Feel:

MIND RESET

I Like To Eat:

I Like To Watch:

I Like To Listen To:

Quotes That Motivate Me:

Bible Scriptures That Motivate Me:

MIND RESET

I'm Getting Used To:

Everyday I Appreciate:

The New Me Looks And Feels:

People I Personally Know With Breast Cancer:

People I Personally Know Who Had Breast Cancer:

MIND RESET

I'm At A Place In My Life Where:

My Attitude Is:

I Imagine Myself:

What I Would Tell Others With Breast Cancer:

I Know I Am:

MIND RESET

Healing Begins:

Healing For Me Feels Like:

I Am Proud Of Myself For:

I Look Forward To:

My Body Is Responding To Treatment:

MIND RESET

My Mind Is Responding To Treatment:

I Have Changed My Life By:

Changes I Am Making Right Now:

One Word That Describes Me:

The Word I Chose As My Answer To The Previous Prompt Means:

MIND RESET

I Do Not Allow My Mind To:

THE CONQUEROR BLUEPRINT

THE CONQUEROR BLUEPRINT

Date:

Today Has Been:

My Body Feels:

I Looked At Myself In The Mirror And Thought:

A Compliment To Myself:

Today I Needed:

I Gave Myself Permission To:

I Feel:

The Best Thing I've Heard Today:

Today I Asked God:

I Thank God For:

Today I Nurtured Myself By:

Today I Laughed At:

Today I:

THE CONQUEROR BLUEPRINT

Date:

Today Has Been:

My Body Feels:

I Looked At Myself In The Mirror And Thought:

A Compliment To Myself:

Today I Needed:

I Gave Myself Permission To:

I Feel:

The Best Thing I've Heard Today:

Today I Asked God:

I Thank God For:

Today I Nurtured Myself By:

Today I Laughed At:

Today I:

I Know That I Am Getting Better.

THE CONQUEROR BLUEPRINT

Date:

I Feel:

Today Has Been:

The Best Thing I've Heard Today:

My Body Feels:

Today I Asked God:

I Looked At Myself In The Mirror And Thought:

I Thank God For:

A Compliment To Myself:

Today I Nurtured Myself By:

Today I Needed:

Today I Laughed At:

I Gave Myself Permission To:

Today I:

I AM STRONGER THAN I LOOK.

NOTHING WILL DEFEAT ME.

THE CONQUEROR BLUEPRINT

Date:

I Feel:

Today Has Been:

The Best Thing I've Heard Today:

My Body Feels:

Today I Asked God:

I Looked At Myself In The Mirror And Thought:

I Thank God For:

A Compliment To Myself:

Today I Nurtured Myself By:

Today I Needed:

Today I Laughed At:

I Gave Myself Permission To:

Today I:

I Am Healing Because I Am Surrounded By Family And Friends Who Love Me.

I AM STRONG ENOUGH TO....

THE CONQUEROR BLUEPRINT

Date:

I Feel:

Today Has Been:

The Best Thing I've Heard Today:

My Body Feels:

Today I Asked God:

I Looked At Myself In The Mirror And Thought:

I Thank God For:

A Compliment To Myself:

Today I Nurtured Myself By:

Today I Needed:

Today I Laughed At:

I Gave Myself Permission To:

Today I:

I Am Focused On Being My Best Self Everyday.

THE CONQUEROR BLUEPRINT

Date: I Feel:

Today Has Been: The Best Thing I've Heard Today:

My Body Feels: Today I Asked God:

I Looked At Myself In The Mirror And   I Thank God For:
Thought:

A Compliment To Myself: Today I Nurtured Myself By:

Today I Needed: Today I Laughed At:

I Gave Myself Permission To: Today I:

MY PERSONAL THOUGHTS

WATCH ME BEAT THIS.

THE CONQUEROR BLUEPRINT

Date:

I Feel:

Today Has Been:

The Best Thing I've Heard Today:

My Body Feels:

Today I Asked God:

I Looked At Myself In The Mirror And Thought:

I Thank God For:

A Compliment To Myself:

Today I Nurtured Myself By:

Today I Needed:

Today I Laughed At:

I Gave Myself Permission To:

Today I:

I Wake Up With A Clear Mind And A Can-Do Attitude.

THE CONQUEROR BLUEPRINT

Date:

I Feel:

Today Has Been:

The Best Thing I've Heard Today:

My Body Feels:

Today I Asked God:

I Looked At Myself In The Mirror And Thought:

I Thank God For:

A Compliment To Myself:

Today I Nurtured Myself By:

Today I Needed:

Today I Laughed At:

I Gave Myself Permission To:

Today I:

WHAT I KNOW ABOUT MYSELF....

THE CONQUEROR BLUEPRINT

Date:

I Feel:

Today Has Been:

The Best Thing I've Heard Today:

My Body Feels:

Today I Asked God:

I Looked At Myself In The Mirror And Thought:

I Thank God For:

A Compliment To Myself:

Today I Nurtured Myself By:

Today I Needed:

Today I Laughed At:

I Gave Myself Permission To:

Today I:

THE CONQUEROR BLUEPRINT

Date: I Feel:

Today Has Been: The Best Thing I've Heard Today:

My Body Feels: Today I Asked God:

I Looked At Myself In The Mirror And   I Thank God For:
Thought:

A Compliment To Myself: Today I Nurtured Myself By:

Today I Needed: Today I Laughed At:

I Gave Myself Permission To: Today I:

In My Healing Journey, I'm Succeeding With The Right Mindset.

THE CONQUEROR BLUEPRINT

Date:

I Feel:

Today Has Been:

The Best Thing I've Heard Today:

My Body Feels:

Today I Asked God:

I Looked At Myself In The Mirror And Thought:

I Thank God For:

A Compliment To Myself:

Today I Nurtured Myself By:

Today I Needed:

Today I Laughed At:

I Gave Myself Permission To:

Today I:

I Am Improving On What I Have - My Health And Wellness.

THIS ISN'T THE FIRST FIGHT THAT I WILL WIN.

THE CONQUEROR BLUEPRINT

Date: I Feel:

Today Has Been: The Best Thing I've Heard Today:

My Body Feels: Today I Asked God:

I Looked At Myself In The Mirror And   I Thank God For:
Thought:

A Compliment To Myself: Today I Nurtured Myself By:

Today I Needed: Today I Laughed At:

I Gave Myself Permission To: Today I:

MY PERSONAL THOUGHTS

MY SPIRIT IS STRONG.

I BELIEVE I AM BEAUTIFUL BECAUSE....

THE CONQUEROR BLUEPRINT

Date: I Feel:

Today Has Been: The Best Thing I've Heard Today:

My Body Feels: Today I Asked God:

I Looked At Myself In The Mirror And   I Thank God For:
Thought:

A Compliment To Myself: Today I Nurtured Myself By:

Today I Needed: Today I Laughed At:

I Gave Myself Permission To: Today I:

THE CONQUEROR BLUEPRINT

Date:

Today Has Been:

My Body Feels:

I Looked At Myself In The Mirror And Thought:

A Compliment To Myself:

Today I Needed:

I Gave Myself Permission To:

I Feel:

The Best Thing I've Heard Today:

Today I Asked God:

I Thank God For:

Today I Nurtured Myself By:

Today I Laughed At:

Today I:

I Am Beautiful And No One Can Take That Fact Away From Me.

THE CONQUEROR BLUEPRINT

Date: I Feel:

Today Has Been: The Best Thing I've Heard Today:

My Body Feels: Today I Asked God:

I Looked At Myself In The Mirror And   I Thank God For:
Thought:

A Compliment To Myself: Today I Nurtured Myself By:

Today I Needed: Today I Laughed At:

I Gave Myself Permission To: Today I:

THE CONQUEROR BLUEPRINT

Date: I Feel:

Today Has Been: The Best Thing I've Heard Today:

My Body Feels: Today I Asked God:

I Looked At Myself In The Mirror And Thought: I Thank God For:

A Compliment To Myself: Today I Nurtured Myself By:

Today I Needed: Today I Laughed At:

I Gave Myself Permission To: Today I:

I WILL DECIDE THE OUTCOME TO THIS.

THE CONQUEROR BLUEPRINT

Date:

I Feel:

Today Has Been:

The Best Thing I've Heard Today:

My Body Feels:

Today I Asked God:

I Looked At Myself In The Mirror And Thought:

I Thank God For:

A Compliment To Myself:

Today I Nurtured Myself By:

Today I Needed:

Today I Laughed At:

I Gave Myself Permission To:

Today I:

I Am Committed To Becoming The Best Version Of Myself.

THE CONQUEROR BLUEPRINT

Date: I Feel:

Today Has Been: The Best Thing I've Heard Today:

My Body Feels: Today I Asked God:

I Looked At Myself In The Mirror And   I Thank God For:
Thought:

A Compliment To Myself: Today I Nurtured Myself By:

Today I Needed: Today I Laughed At:

I Gave Myself Permission To: Today I:

THE CONQUEROR BLUEPRINT

Date: I Feel:

Today Has Been: The Best Thing I've Heard Today:

My Body Feels: Today I Asked God:

I Looked At Myself In The Mirror And   I Thank God For:
Thought:

A Compliment To Myself: Today I Nurtured Myself By:

Today I Needed: Today I Laughed At:

I Gave Myself Permission To: Today I:

This Challenge Hasn't Broken My Spirit. It Has Made Me Stronger.

THE CONQUEROR BLUEPRINT

Date: I Feel:

Today Has Been: The Best Thing I've Heard Today:

My Body Feels: Today I Asked God:

I Looked At Myself In The Mirror And   I Thank God For:
Thought:

A Compliment To Myself: Today I Nurtured Myself By:

Today I Needed: Today I Laughed At:

I Gave Myself Permission To: Today I:

THIS PAIN IS ONLY MAKING ME STRONGER.

MY BOOBIES ARE LOVELY ANYWAY THAT THEY ARE.

THE CONQUEROR BLUEPRINT

Date: | I Feel:

Today Has Been: | The Best Thing I've Heard Today:

My Body Feels: | Today I Asked God:

I Looked At Myself In The Mirror And Thought: | I Thank God For:

A Compliment To Myself: | Today I Nurtured Myself By:

Today I Needed: | Today I Laughed At:

I Gave Myself Permission To: | Today I:

THE CONQUEROR BLUEPRINT

Date: I Feel:

Today Has Been: The Best Thing I've Heard Today:

My Body Feels: Today I Asked God:

I Looked At Myself In The Mirror And   I Thank God For:
Thought:

A Compliment To Myself: Today I Nurtured Myself By:

Today I Needed: Today I Laughed At:

I Gave Myself Permission To: Today I:

MY PERSONAL THOUGHTS

THE CONQUEROR BLUEPRINT

Date: I Feel:

Today Has Been: The Best Thing I've Heard Today:

My Body Feels: Today I Asked God:

I Looked At Myself In The Mirror And   I Thank God For:
Thought:

A Compliment To Myself: Today I Nurtured Myself By:

Today I Needed: Today I Laughed At:

I Gave Myself Permission To: Today I:

THE CONQUEROR BLUEPRINT

Date: I Feel:

Today Has Been: The Best Thing I've Heard Today:

My Body Feels: Today I Asked God:

I Looked At Myself In The Mirror And Thought: I Thank God For:

A Compliment To Myself: Today I Nurtured Myself By:

Today I Needed: Today I Laughed At:

I Gave Myself Permission To: Today I:

THE CONQUEROR BLUEPRINT

Date: I Feel:

Today Has Been: The Best Thing I've Heard Today:

My Body Feels: Today I Asked God:

I Looked At Myself In The Mirror And   I Thank God For:
Thought:

A Compliment To Myself: Today I Nurtured Myself By:

Today I Needed: Today I Laughed At:

I Gave Myself Permission To: Today I:

THE CONQUEROR BLUEPRINT

Date:

I Feel:

Today Has Been:

The Best Thing I've Heard Today:

My Body Feels:

Today I Asked God:

I Looked At Myself In The Mirror And Thought:

I Thank God For:

A Compliment To Myself:

Today I Nurtured Myself By:

Today I Needed:

Today I Laughed At:

I Gave Myself Permission To:

Today I:

I Wake Up Feeling Stronger In My Heart, Body And Mind.

DEAR GOD, MAY EVERY CANCER CELL BE DESTROYED.

I VIEW MY BREAST AS....

THE CONQUEROR BLUEPRINT

Date: I Feel:

Today Has Been: The Best Thing I've Heard Today:

My Body Feels: Today I Asked God:

I Looked At Myself In The Mirror And   I Thank God For:
Thought:

A Compliment To Myself: Today I Nurtured Myself By:

Today I Needed: Today I Laughed At:

I Gave Myself Permission To: Today I:

THE CONQUEROR BLUEPRINT

Date: I Feel:

Today Has Been: The Best Thing I've Heard Today:

My Body Feels: Today I Asked God:

I Looked At Myself In The Mirror And   I Thank God For:
Thought:

A Compliment To Myself: Today I Nurtured Myself By:

Today I Needed: Today I Laughed At:

I Gave Myself Permission To: Today I:

I Welcome All The People, Things, Events, And Circumstances That Will Help Me Heal And Grow.

THE CONQUEROR BLUEPRINT

Date: I Feel:

Today Has Been: The Best Thing I've Heard Today:

My Body Feels: Today I Asked God:

I Looked At Myself In The Mirror And   I Thank God For:
Thought:

A Compliment To Myself: Today I Nurtured Myself By:

Today I Needed: Today I Laughed At:

I Gave Myself Permission To: Today I:

I'M NOT FIGHTING THIS ON MY OWN.

MY MINDSET IS MY BIGGEST WEAPON.

THE CONQUEROR BLUEPRINT

Date: I Feel:

Today Has Been: The Best Thing I've Heard Today:

My Body Feels: Today I Asked God:

I Looked At Myself In The Mirror And   I Thank God For:
Thought:

A Compliment To Myself: Today I Nurtured Myself By:

Today I Needed: Today I Laughed At:

I Gave Myself Permission To: Today I:

I Am Deciding To Get Well. I Am Deciding To Be Well.

THE CONQUEROR BLUEPRINT

Date: I Feel:

Today Has Been: The Best Thing I've Heard Today:

My Body Feels: Today I Asked God:

I Looked At Myself In The Mirror And I Thank God For:
Thought:

A Compliment To Myself: Today I Nurtured Myself By:

Today I Needed: Today I Laughed At:

I Gave Myself Permission To: Today I:

THE CONQUEROR BLUEPRINT

Date:

I Feel:

Today Has Been:

The Best Thing I've Heard Today:

My Body Feels:

Today I Asked God:

I Looked At Myself In The Mirror And Thought:

I Thank God For:

A Compliment To Myself:

Today I Nurtured Myself By:

Today I Needed:

Today I Laughed At:

I Gave Myself Permission To:

Today I:

I Proudly Wear My Scars To Remind Me Of My Successful Wins.

MY PERSONAL THOUGHTS

THE CONQUEROR BLUEPRINT

Date:

I Feel:

Today Has Been:

The Best Thing I've Heard Today:

My Body Feels:

Today I Asked God:

I Looked At Myself In The Mirror And Thought:

I Thank God For:

A Compliment To Myself:

Today I Nurtured Myself By:

Today I Needed:

Today I Laughed At:

I Gave Myself Permission To:

Today I:

My Body Grows Stronger Every Day.

THE CONQUEROR BLUEPRINT

Date: I Feel:

Today Has Been: The Best Thing I've Heard Today:

My Body Feels: Today I Asked God:

I Looked At Myself In The Mirror And   I Thank God For:
Thought:

A Compliment To Myself: Today I Nurtured Myself By:

Today I Needed: Today I Laughed At:

I Gave Myself Permission To: Today I:

I Am Blessed To Be Handed A Second, Third, And Fourth Chance.

THE CONQUEROR BLUEPRINT

Date:

Today Has Been:

My Body Feels:

I Looked At Myself In The Mirror And Thought:

A Compliment To Myself:

Today I Needed:

I Gave Myself Permission To:

I Feel:

The Best Thing I've Heard Today:

Today I Asked God:

I Thank God For:

Today I Nurtured Myself By:

Today I Laughed At:

Today I:

I Can Rise Above Any Obstacle Because I Have Faith.

WHAT KEEPS ME GOING?

I'M SHOWING OTHERS HOW TO BEAT THIS THING.

THE CONQUEROR BLUEPRINT

Date:

I Feel:

Today Has Been:

The Best Thing I've Heard Today:

My Body Feels:

Today I Asked God:

I Looked At Myself In The Mirror And Thought:

I Thank God For:

A Compliment To Myself:

Today I Nurtured Myself By:

Today I Needed:

Today I Laughed At:

I Gave Myself Permission To:

Today I:

THE CONQUEROR BLUEPRINT

Date:

I Feel:

Today Has Been:

The Best Thing I've Heard Today:

My Body Feels:

Today I Asked God:

I Looked At Myself In The Mirror And Thought:

I Thank God For:

A Compliment To Myself:

Today I Nurtured Myself By:

Today I Needed:

Today I Laughed At:

I Gave Myself Permission To:

Today I:

THE CONQUEROR BLUEPRINT

Date: I Feel:

Today Has Been: The Best Thing I've Heard Today:

My Body Feels: Today I Asked God:

I Looked At Myself In The Mirror And   I Thank God For:
Thought:

A Compliment To Myself: Today I Nurtured Myself By:

Today I Needed: Today I Laughed At:

I Gave Myself Permission To: Today I:

MY PERSONAL THOUGHTS

GOD HAS SOMETHING SO SPECIAL SET UP FOR ME.

THE CONQUEROR BLUEPRINT

Date:

I Feel:

Today Has Been:

The Best Thing I've Heard Today:

My Body Feels:

Today I Asked God:

I Looked At Myself In The Mirror And Thought:

I Thank God For:

A Compliment To Myself:

Today I Nurtured Myself By:

Today I Needed:

Today I Laughed At:

I Gave Myself Permission To:

Today I:

THE CONQUEROR BLUEPRINT

Date:

I Feel:

Today Has Been:

The Best Thing I've Heard Today:

My Body Feels:

Today I Asked God:

I Looked At Myself In The Mirror And Thought:

I Thank God For:

A Compliment To Myself:

Today I Nurtured Myself By:

Today I Needed:

Today I Laughed At:

I Gave Myself Permission To:

Today I:

THE CONQUEROR BLUEPRINT

Date:

I Feel:

Today Has Been:

The Best Thing I've Heard Today:

My Body Feels:

Today I Asked God:

I Looked At Myself In The Mirror And Thought:

I Thank God For:

A Compliment To Myself:

Today I Nurtured Myself By:

Today I Needed:

Today I Laughed At:

I Gave Myself Permission To:

Today I:

I See Myself Breast Cancer Free.

THE CONQUEROR BLUEPRINT

Date: I Feel:

Today Has Been: The Best Thing I've Heard Today:

My Body Feels: Today I Asked God:

I Looked At Myself In The Mirror And   I Thank God For:
Thought:

A Compliment To Myself: Today I Nurtured Myself By:

Today I Needed: Today I Laughed At:

I Gave Myself Permission To: Today I:

THE CONQUEROR BLUEPRINT

Date: I Feel:

Today Has Been: The Best Thing I've Heard Today:

My Body Feels: Today I Asked God:

I Looked At Myself In The Mirror And   I Thank God For:
Thought:

A Compliment To Myself: Today I Nurtured Myself By:

Today I Needed: Today I Laughed At:

I Gave Myself Permission To: Today I:

I Breath Deeply, Bringing Energy To All My Cells.

NO WEAPON FORMED AGAINST YOU SHALL PROSPER.
- ISAIAH 54:17

THE CONQUEROR BLUEPRINT

Date:

I Feel:

Today Has Been:

The Best Thing I've Heard Today:

My Body Feels:

Today I Asked God:

I Looked At Myself In The Mirror And Thought:

I Thank God For:

A Compliment To Myself:

Today I Nurtured Myself By:

Today I Needed:

Today I Laughed At:

I Gave Myself Permission To:

Today I:

I Am Alive, And I Still Have A Glorious Purpose.

THE CONQUEROR BLUEPRINT

Date:

I Feel:

Today Has Been:

The Best Thing I've Heard Today:

My Body Feels:

Today I Asked God:

I Looked At Myself In The Mirror And Thought:

I Thank God For:

A Compliment To Myself:

Today I Nurtured Myself By:

Today I Needed:

Today I Laughed At:

I Gave Myself Permission To:

Today I:

THE CONQUEROR BLUEPRINT

Date:

I Feel:

Today Has Been:

The Best Thing I've Heard Today:

My Body Feels:

Today I Asked God:

I Looked At Myself In The Mirror And Thought:

I Thank God For:

A Compliment To Myself:

Today I Nurtured Myself By:

Today I Needed:

Today I Laughed At:

I Gave Myself Permission To:

Today I:

I'm An Amazing Woman, And There's Always Something To Live For.

THE CONQUEROR BLUEPRINT

Date: I Feel:

Today Has Been: The Best Thing I've Heard Today:

My Body Feels: Today I Asked God:

I Looked At Myself In The Mirror And   I Thank God For:
Thought:

A Compliment To Myself: Today I Nurtured Myself By:

Today I Needed: Today I Laughed At:

I Gave Myself Permission To: Today I:

CANCER IS CANCELLED.

I SEE MYSELF HAPPY, HEALTHY AND BEAUTIFUL.

THE CONQUEROR BLUEPRINT

Date: I Feel:

Today Has Been: The Best Thing I've Heard Today:

My Body Feels: Today I Asked God:

I Looked At Myself In The Mirror And   I Thank God For:
Thought:

A Compliment To Myself: Today I Nurtured Myself By:

Today I Needed: Today I Laughed At:

I Gave Myself Permission To: Today I:

THE CONQUEROR BLUEPRINT

Date: I Feel:

Today Has Been: The Best Thing I've Heard Today:

My Body Feels: Today I Asked God:

I Looked At Myself In The Mirror And   I Thank God For:
Thought:

A Compliment To Myself: Today I Nurtured Myself By:

Today I Needed: Today I Laughed At:

I Gave Myself Permission To: Today I:

THE CONQUEROR BLUEPRINT

Date: I Feel:

Today Has Been: The Best Thing I've Heard Today:

My Body Feels: Today I Asked God:

I Looked At Myself In The Mirror And   I Thank God For:
Thought:

A Compliment To Myself: Today I Nurtured Myself By:

Today I Needed: Today I Laughed At:

I Gave Myself Permission To: Today I:

I Deserve To Heal. I Am Ready.

THE CONQUEROR BLUEPRINT

Date: | I Feel:

Today Has Been: | The Best Thing I've Heard Today:

My Body Feels: | Today I Asked God:

I Looked At Myself In The Mirror And Thought: | I Thank God For:

A Compliment To Myself: | Today I Nurtured Myself By:

Today I Needed: | Today I Laughed At:

I Gave Myself Permission To: | Today I:

As A Superhero, I Can Face Challenges And Emerge Victorious.

THIS TOO SHALL PASS.

I'M ALWAYS IN THE MOOD TO FEEL BETTER.

THE CONQUEROR BLUEPRINT

Date: I Feel:

Today Has Been: The Best Thing I've Heard Today:

My Body Feels: Today I Asked God:

I Looked At Myself In The Mirror And   I Thank God For:
Thought:

A Compliment To Myself: Today I Nurtured Myself By:

Today I Needed: Today I Laughed At:

I Gave Myself Permission To: Today I:

I Am The Owner Of A Cancer Free Mind And Body.

THE CONQUEROR BLUEPRINT

Date: I Feel:

Today Has Been: The Best Thing I've Heard Today:

My Body Feels: Today I Asked God:

I Looked At Myself In The Mirror And   I Thank God For:
Thought:

A Compliment To Myself: Today I Nurtured Myself By:

Today I Needed: Today I Laughed At:

I Gave Myself Permission To: Today I:

THE CONQUEROR BLUEPRINT

Date: I Feel:

Today Has Been: The Best Thing I've Heard Today:

My Body Feels: Today I Asked God:

I Looked At Myself In The Mirror And   I Thank God For:
Thought:

A Compliment To Myself: Today I Nurtured Myself By:

Today I Needed: Today I Laughed At:

I Gave Myself Permission To: Today I:

My First Goal In Recovery Is Eating More Delicious Vegetables.

I BELIEVE GOD IS USING ME FOR....

THE CONQUEROR BLUEPRINT

Date:

Today Has Been:

My Body Feels:

I Looked At Myself In The Mirror And Thought:

A Compliment To Myself:

Today I Needed:

I Gave Myself Permission To:

I Feel:

The Best Thing I've Heard Today:

Today I Asked God:

I Thank God For:

Today I Nurtured Myself By:

Today I Laughed At:

Today I:

I Only Surround Myself With People Who Believe I Will Beat Breast Cancer.

THE CONQUEROR BLUEPRINT

Date:

I Feel:

Today Has Been:

The Best Thing I've Heard Today:

My Body Feels:

Today I Asked God:

I Looked At Myself In The Mirror And Thought:

I Thank God For:

A Compliment To Myself:

Today I Nurtured Myself By:

Today I Needed:

Today I Laughed At:

I Gave Myself Permission To:

Today I:

THE CONQUEROR BLUEPRINT

Date: I Feel:

Today Has Been: The Best Thing I've Heard Today:

My Body Feels: Today I Asked God:

I Looked At Myself In The Mirror And   I Thank God For:
Thought:

A Compliment To Myself: Today I Nurtured Myself By:

Today I Needed: Today I Laughed At:

I Gave Myself Permission To: Today I:

Nothing Can Hold Me Down. Nothing.

CHANGES TO MY PHYSICAL APPEARANCE.....

THE CONQUEROR BLUEPRINT

Date: I Feel:

Today Has Been: The Best Thing I've Heard Today:

My Body Feels: Today I Asked God:

I Looked At Myself In The Mirror And   I Thank God For:
Thought:

A Compliment To Myself: Today I Nurtured Myself By:

Today I Needed: Today I Laughed At:

I Gave Myself Permission To: Today I:

My Body Deserves Love And Respect.

THE CONQUEROR BLUEPRINT

Date:

I Feel:

Today Has Been:

The Best Thing I've Heard Today:

My Body Feels:

Today I Asked God:

I Looked At Myself In The Mirror And Thought:

I Thank God For:

A Compliment To Myself:

Today I Nurtured Myself By:

Today I Needed:

Today I Laughed At:

I Gave Myself Permission To:

Today I:

I'm Positive That My Best Years Are Still Ahead Of Me.

MY HEART IS FILLED WITH HOPE.

THERE IS A MIRACLE HAPPENING RIGHT NOW.

THE CONQUEROR BLUEPRINT

Date:

I Feel:

Today Has Been:

The Best Thing I've Heard Today:

My Body Feels:

Today I Asked God:

I Looked At Myself In The Mirror And Thought:

I Thank God For:

A Compliment To Myself:

Today I Nurtured Myself By:

Today I Needed:

Today I Laughed At:

I Gave Myself Permission To:

Today I:

I Honor My Need To Rest And Recharge.

THE CONQUEROR BLUEPRINT

Date: I Feel:

Today Has Been: The Best Thing I've Heard Today:

My Body Feels: Today I Asked God:

I Looked At Myself In The Mirror And   I Thank God For:
Thought:

A Compliment To Myself: Today I Nurtured Myself By:

Today I Needed: Today I Laughed At:

I Gave Myself Permission To: Today I:

THE CONQUEROR BLUEPRINT

Date: I Feel:

Today Has Been: The Best Thing I've Heard Today:

My Body Feels: Today I Asked God:

I Looked At Myself In The Mirror And   I Thank God For:
Thought:

A Compliment To Myself: Today I Nurtured Myself By:

Today I Needed: Today I Laughed At:

I Gave Myself Permission To: Today I:

MY PERSONAL THOUGHTS

FIVE BIBLE VERSES THAT I KEEP CLOSE TO MY HEART....

THE CONQUEROR BLUEPRINT

Date:

I Feel:

Today Has Been:

The Best Thing I've Heard Today:

My Body Feels:

Today I Asked God:

I Looked At Myself In The Mirror And Thought:

I Thank God For:

A Compliment To Myself:

Today I Nurtured Myself By:

Today I Needed:

Today I Laughed At:

I Gave Myself Permission To:

Today I:

THE CONQUEROR BLUEPRINT

Date: I Feel:

Today Has Been: The Best Thing I've Heard Today:

My Body Feels: Today I Asked God:

I Looked At Myself In The Mirror And Thought: I Thank God For:

A Compliment To Myself: Today I Nurtured Myself By:

Today I Needed: Today I Laughed At:

I Gave Myself Permission To: Today I:

THE CONQUEROR BLUEPRINT

Date:

I Feel:

Today Has Been:

The Best Thing I've Heard Today:

My Body Feels:

Today I Asked God:

I Looked At Myself In The Mirror And Thought:

I Thank God For:

A Compliment To Myself:

Today I Nurtured Myself By:

Today I Needed:

Today I Laughed At:

I Gave Myself Permission To:

Today I:

THIS IS A TIME OF RECOVERY.

THERE IS SOMETHING GOOD IN MY TODAY.

THE CONQUEROR BLUEPRINT

Date: I Feel:

Today Has Been: The Best Thing I've Heard Today:

My Body Feels: Today I Asked God:

I Looked At Myself In The Mirror And   I Thank God For:
Thought:

A Compliment To Myself: Today I Nurtured Myself By:

Today I Needed: Today I Laughed At:

I Gave Myself Permission To: Today I:

THE CONQUEROR BLUEPRINT

Date: I Feel:

Today Has Been: The Best Thing I've Heard Today:

My Body Feels: Today I Asked God:

I Looked At Myself In The Mirror And   I Thank God For:
Thought:

A Compliment To Myself: Today I Nurtured Myself By:

Today I Needed: Today I Laughed At:

I Gave Myself Permission To: Today I:

THE CONQUEROR BLUEPRINT

Date: I Feel:

Today Has Been: The Best Thing I've Heard Today:

My Body Feels: Today I Asked God:

I Looked At Myself In The Mirror And   I Thank God For:
Thought:

A Compliment To Myself: Today I Nurtured Myself By:

Today I Needed: Today I Laughed At:

I Gave Myself Permission To: Today I:

I Am Positively Designing My Life To Revolve Around Love.

10 SONGS THAT RAISE MY SPIRITS....

I'M LEARNING A LOT MORE ABOUT MYSELF THROUGH ALL THIS PAIN.

THE CONQUEROR BLUEPRINT

Date: I Feel:

Today Has Been: The Best Thing I've Heard Today:

My Body Feels: Today I Asked God:

I Looked At Myself In The Mirror And   I Thank God For:
Thought:

A Compliment To Myself: Today I Nurtured Myself By:

Today I Needed: Today I Laughed At:

I Gave Myself Permission To: Today I:

THE CONQUEROR BLUEPRINT

Date:

I Feel:

Today Has Been:

The Best Thing I've Heard Today:

My Body Feels:

Today I Asked God:

I Looked At Myself In The Mirror And Thought:

I Thank God For:

A Compliment To Myself:

Today I Nurtured Myself By:

Today I Needed:

Today I Laughed At:

I Gave Myself Permission To:

Today I:

I Accept Myself Just As I Am.

THE CONQUEROR BLUEPRINT

Date:

I Feel:

Today Has Been:

The Best Thing I've Heard Today:

My Body Feels:

Today I Asked God:

I Looked At Myself In The Mirror And Thought:

I Thank God For:

A Compliment To Myself:

Today I Nurtured Myself By:

Today I Needed:

Today I Laughed At:

I Gave Myself Permission To:

Today I:

HEALING BEGINS....

GOD SAID ALL THINGS WILL WORK OUT FOR MY GOOD.

THE CONQUEROR BLUEPRINT

Date:

Today Has Been:

My Body Feels:

I Looked At Myself In The Mirror And Thought:

A Compliment To Myself:

Today I Needed:

I Gave Myself Permission To:

I Feel:

The Best Thing I've Heard Today:

Today I Asked God:

I Thank God For:

Today I Nurtured Myself By:

Today I Laughed At:

Today I:

I'm Saying It Out Loud That I Will Beat Breast Cancer.

THE CONQUEROR BLUEPRINT

Date:

I Feel:

Today Has Been:

The Best Thing I've Heard Today:

My Body Feels:

Today I Asked God:

I Looked At Myself In The Mirror And Thought:

I Thank God For:

A Compliment To Myself:

Today I Nurtured Myself By:

Today I Needed:

Today I Laughed At:

I Gave Myself Permission To:

Today I:

Every Cell In My Body Is Healthy And Well.

THE CONQUEROR BLUEPRINT

Date: I Feel:

Today Has Been: The Best Thing I've Heard Today:

My Body Feels: Today I Asked God:

I Looked At Myself In The Mirror And   I Thank God For:
Thought:

A Compliment To Myself: Today I Nurtured Myself By:

Today I Needed: Today I Laughed At:

I Gave Myself Permission To: Today I:

WHAT CURRENTLY MAKES ME HAPPY?

I'M A DIFFERENT WOMAN NOW. I AM A BETTER WOMAN NOW.

THE CONQUEROR BLUEPRINT

Date: I Feel:

Today Has Been: The Best Thing I've Heard Today:

My Body Feels: Today I Asked God:

I Looked At Myself In The Mirror And   I Thank God For:
Thought:

A Compliment To Myself: Today I Nurtured Myself By:

Today I Needed: Today I Laughed At:

I Gave Myself Permission To: Today I:

THE CONQUEROR BLUEPRINT

Date: I Feel:

Today Has Been: The Best Thing I've Heard Today:

My Body Feels: Today I Asked God:

I Looked At Myself In The Mirror And Thought: I Thank God For:

A Compliment To Myself: Today I Nurtured Myself By:

Today I Needed: Today I Laughed At:

I Gave Myself Permission To: Today I:

THE CONQUEROR BLUEPRINT

Date: I Feel:

Today Has Been: The Best Thing I've Heard Today:

My Body Feels: Today I Asked God:

I Looked At Myself In The Mirror And   I Thank God For:
Thought:

A Compliment To Myself: Today I Nurtured Myself By:

Today I Needed: Today I Laughed At:

I Gave Myself Permission To: Today I:

THE TRUTH ABOUT BREAST CANCER IS....

I AM HERE FOR ME.

THE CONQUEROR BLUEPRINT

Date: I Feel:

Today Has Been: The Best Thing I've Heard Today:

My Body Feels: Today I Asked God:

I Looked At Myself In The Mirror And   I Thank God For:
Thought:

A Compliment To Myself: Today I Nurtured Myself By:

Today I Needed: Today I Laughed At:

I Gave Myself Permission To: Today I:

I Only Create Good Things For Myself.

THE CONQUEROR BLUEPRINT

Date: I Feel:

Today Has Been: The Best Thing I've Heard Today:

My Body Feels: Today I Asked God:

I Looked At Myself In The Mirror And   I Thank God For:
Thought:

A Compliment To Myself: Today I Nurtured Myself By:

Today I Needed: Today I Laughed At:

I Gave Myself Permission To: Today I:

THE CONQUEROR BLUEPRINT

Date:

Today Has Been:

My Body Feels:

I Looked At Myself In The Mirror And Thought:

A Compliment To Myself:

Today I Needed:

I Gave Myself Permission To:

I Feel:

The Best Thing I've Heard Today:

Today I Asked God:

I Thank God For:

Today I Nurtured Myself By:

Today I Laughed At:

Today I:

Faith And Love From Others Can Help Me Conquer This.

THE CONQUEROR BLUEPRINT

Date:

I Feel:

Today Has Been:

The Best Thing I've Heard Today:

My Body Feels:

Today I Asked God:

I Looked At Myself In The Mirror And Thought:

I Thank God For:

A Compliment To Myself:

Today I Nurtured Myself By:

Today I Needed:

Today I Laughed At:

I Gave Myself Permission To:

Today I:

IT DOESN'T MATTER WHO IS HERE WITH YOU WHEN ALL YOU NEED IS YOU.

DEAR BODY, I PROMISE TO LOVE AND CHERISH YOU ALWAYS.

THE CONQUEROR BLUEPRINT

Date: I Feel:

Today Has Been: The Best Thing I've Heard Today:

My Body Feels: Today I Asked God:

I Looked At Myself In The Mirror And   I Thank God For:
Thought:

A Compliment To Myself: Today I Nurtured Myself By:

Today I Needed: Today I Laughed At:

I Gave Myself Permission To: Today I:

My Recovery Journey Is About Having People I Trust Around Me.

THE CONQUEROR BLUEPRINT

Date: I Feel:

Today Has Been: The Best Thing I've Heard Today:

My Body Feels: Today I Asked God:

I Looked At Myself In The Mirror And   I Thank God For:
Thought:

A Compliment To Myself: Today I Nurtured Myself By:

Today I Needed: Today I Laughed At:

I Gave Myself Permission To: Today I:

THE CONQUEROR BLUEPRINT

Date: I Feel:

Today Has Been: The Best Thing I've Heard Today:

My Body Feels: Today I Asked God:

I Looked At Myself In The Mirror And   I Thank God For:
Thought:

A Compliment To Myself: Today I Nurtured Myself By:

Today I Needed: Today I Laughed At:

I Gave Myself Permission To: Today I:

I LIKE TO KEEP PEOPLE AROUND ME WHO....

I'M NOT IN THIS FIGHT BECAUSE I'M WEAK. I'M IN THIS FIGHT BECAUSE IT'S TIME TO EXERCISE THE STRENGTH WITHIN ME.

THE CONQUEROR BLUEPRINT

Date: I Feel:

Today Has Been: The Best Thing I've Heard Today:

My Body Feels: Today I Asked God:

I Looked At Myself In The Mirror And   I Thank God For:
Thought:

A Compliment To Myself: Today I Nurtured Myself By:

Today I Needed: Today I Laughed At:

I Gave Myself Permission To: Today I:

THE CONQUEROR BLUEPRINT

Date: I Feel:

Today Has Been: The Best Thing I've Heard Today:

My Body Feels: Today I Asked God:

I Looked At Myself In The Mirror And   I Thank God For:
Thought:

A Compliment To Myself: Today I Nurtured Myself By:

Today I Needed: Today I Laughed At:

I Gave Myself Permission To: Today I:

THE CONQUEROR BLUEPRINT

Date:

I Feel:

Today Has Been:

The Best Thing I've Heard Today:

My Body Feels:

Today I Asked God:

I Looked At Myself In The Mirror And Thought:

I Thank God For:

A Compliment To Myself:

Today I Nurtured Myself By:

Today I Needed:

Today I Laughed At:

I Gave Myself Permission To:

Today I:

I AM GOING TO USE THIS TIME IN MY LIFE TO....

THIS WILL NOT BREAK ME.

THE CONQUEROR BLUEPRINT

Date:

I Feel:

Today Has Been:

The Best Thing I've Heard Today:

My Body Feels:

Today I Asked God:

I Looked At Myself In The Mirror And Thought:

I Thank God For:

A Compliment To Myself:

Today I Nurtured Myself By:

Today I Needed:

Today I Laughed At:

I Gave Myself Permission To:

Today I:

I Am Being Taught Gratitude. My Gratitude Is Expanding.

THE CONQUEROR BLUEPRINT

Date:

I Feel:

Today Has Been:

The Best Thing I've Heard Today:

My Body Feels:

Today I Asked God:

I Looked At Myself In The Mirror And Thought:

I Thank God For:

A Compliment To Myself:

Today I Nurtured Myself By:

Today I Needed:

Today I Laughed At:

I Gave Myself Permission To:

Today I:

My Faith Is Bigger Than This Sickness.

THE CONQUEROR BLUEPRINT

Date:

I Feel:

Today Has Been:

The Best Thing I've Heard Today:

My Body Feels:

Today I Asked God:

I Looked At Myself In The Mirror And Thought:

I Thank God For:

A Compliment To Myself:

Today I Nurtured Myself By:

Today I Needed:

Today I Laughed At:

I Gave Myself Permission To:

Today I:

I Am Handling This Adversity With Strength, Faith And Determination.

QUESTIONS I HAVE ASKED MYSELF....

I WANT PEOPLE AROUND ME WHO SEE ME AT MY WORST AND STILL BELIEVE I'M AT MY BEST.

THE CONQUEROR BLUEPRINT

Date: I Feel:

Today Has Been: The Best Thing I've Heard Today:

My Body Feels: Today I Asked God:

I Looked At Myself In The Mirror And   I Thank God For:
Thought:

A Compliment To Myself: Today I Nurtured Myself By:

Today I Needed: Today I Laughed At:

I Gave Myself Permission To: Today I:

THE CONQUEROR BLUEPRINT

Date: I Feel:

Today Has Been: The Best Thing I've Heard Today:

My Body Feels: Today I Asked God:

I Looked At Myself In The Mirror And   I Thank God For:
Thought:

A Compliment To Myself: Today I Nurtured Myself By:

Today I Needed: Today I Laughed At:

I Gave Myself Permission To: Today I:

THE CONQUEROR BLUEPRINT

Date:

I Feel:

Today Has Been:

The Best Thing I've Heard Today:

My Body Feels:

Today I Asked God:

I Looked At Myself In The Mirror And Thought:

I Thank God For:

A Compliment To Myself:

Today I Nurtured Myself By:

Today I Needed:

Today I Laughed At:

I Gave Myself Permission To:

Today I:

MY PERSONAL THOUGHTS

IT DOESN'T MATTER WHAT THE ODDS ARE, THERE WILL ALWAYS BE HOPE.

THE CONQUEROR BLUEPRINT

Date:

I Feel:

Today Has Been:

The Best Thing I've Heard Today:

My Body Feels:

Today I Asked God:

I Looked At Myself In The Mirror And Thought:

I Thank God For:

A Compliment To Myself:

Today I Nurtured Myself By:

Today I Needed:

Today I Laughed At:

I Gave Myself Permission To:

Today I:

I Am A Magnet For Healing Energy And Good Feelings.

THE CONQUEROR BLUEPRINT

Date:

I Feel:

Today Has Been:

The Best Thing I've Heard Today:

My Body Feels:

Today I Asked God:

I Looked At Myself In The Mirror And Thought:

I Thank God For:

A Compliment To Myself:

Today I Nurtured Myself By:

Today I Needed:

Today I Laughed At:

I Gave Myself Permission To:

Today I:

I Am A Ray Of Light To My Loved Ones.

THE CONQUEROR BLUEPRINT

Date:

I Feel:

Today Has Been:

The Best Thing I've Heard Today:

My Body Feels:

Today I Asked God:

I Looked At Myself In The Mirror And Thought:

I Thank God For:

A Compliment To Myself:

Today I Nurtured Myself By:

Today I Needed:

Today I Laughed At:

I Gave Myself Permission To:

Today I:

20 WAYS I AM NURTURING MYSELF....

CANCER THOUGHT IT WAS GOING TO BEAT ME. IT'S STARTING TO REALIZE IT'S LOSING THE FIGHT.

THE CONQUEROR BLUEPRINT

Date:

I Feel:

Today Has Been:

The Best Thing I've Heard Today:

My Body Feels:

Today I Asked God:

I Looked At Myself In The Mirror And Thought:

I Thank God For:

A Compliment To Myself:

Today I Nurtured Myself By:

Today I Needed:

Today I Laughed At:

I Gave Myself Permission To:

Today I:

THE CONQUEROR BLUEPRINT

Date:

I Feel:

Today Has Been:

The Best Thing I've Heard Today:

My Body Feels:

Today I Asked God:

I Looked At Myself In The Mirror And Thought:

I Thank God For:

A Compliment To Myself:

Today I Nurtured Myself By:

Today I Needed:

Today I Laughed At:

I Gave Myself Permission To:

Today I:

Thank You For My Friends Who Remind Me That I'm Awesome.

THE CONQUEROR BLUEPRINT

Date:

I Feel:

Today Has Been:

The Best Thing I've Heard Today:

My Body Feels:

Today I Asked God:

I Looked At Myself In The Mirror And Thought:

I Thank God For:

A Compliment To Myself:

Today I Nurtured Myself By:

Today I Needed:

Today I Laughed At:

I Gave Myself Permission To:

Today I:

MY PERSONAL THOUGHTS

THE CONQUEROR BLUEPRINT

Date:

I Feel:

Today Has Been:

The Best Thing I've Heard Today:

My Body Feels:

Today I Asked God:

I Looked At Myself In The Mirror And Thought:

I Thank God For:

A Compliment To Myself:

Today I Nurtured Myself By:

Today I Needed:

Today I Laughed At:

I Gave Myself Permission To:

Today I:

THE CONQUEROR BLUEPRINT

Date: I Feel:

Today Has Been: The Best Thing I've Heard Today:

My Body Feels: Today I Asked God:

I Looked At Myself In The Mirror And   I Thank God For:
Thought:

A Compliment To Myself: Today I Nurtured Myself By:

Today I Needed: Today I Laughed At:

I Gave Myself Permission To: Today I:

THE CONQUEROR BLUEPRINT

Date: I Feel:

Today Has Been: The Best Thing I've Heard Today:

My Body Feels: Today I Asked God:

I Looked At Myself In The Mirror And   I Thank God For:
Thought:

A Compliment To Myself: Today I Nurtured Myself By:

Today I Needed: Today I Laughed At:

I Gave Myself Permission To: Today I:

HELLO STRONG WOMAN, THINGS ARE GETTING BRIGHTER.

15 STRENGTHS I POSSESS....

THE CONQUEROR BLUEPRINT

Date: I Feel:

Today Has Been: | The Best Thing I've Heard Today:

My Body Feels: | Today I Asked God:

I Looked At Myself In The Mirror And Thought: | I Thank God For:

A Compliment To Myself: | Today I Nurtured Myself By:

Today I Needed: | Today I Laughed At:

I Gave Myself Permission To: | Today I:

I Am Radiating With Gratitude, Joy, Love, And Perfect Health.

THE CONQUEROR BLUEPRINT

Date: I Feel:

Today Has Been: The Best Thing I've Heard Today:

My Body Feels: Today I Asked God:

I Looked At Myself In The Mirror And   I Thank God For:
Thought:

A Compliment To Myself: Today I Nurtured Myself By:

Today I Needed: Today I Laughed At:

I Gave Myself Permission To: Today I:

I Take Great Care Of Myself.

THE CONQUEROR BLUEPRINT

Date:

I Feel:

Today Has Been:

The Best Thing I've Heard Today:

My Body Feels:

Today I Asked God:

I Looked At Myself In The Mirror And Thought:

I Thank God For:

A Compliment To Myself:

Today I Nurtured Myself By:

Today I Needed:

Today I Laughed At:

I Gave Myself Permission To:

Today I:

I Am Energized To Approach My Therapy With A Positive Attitude.

MY PERSONAL THOUGHTS

THE CONQUEROR BLUEPRINT

Date:

I Feel:

Today Has Been:

The Best Thing I've Heard Today:

My Body Feels:

Today I Asked God:

I Looked At Myself In The Mirror And Thought:

I Thank God For:

A Compliment To Myself:

Today I Nurtured Myself By:

Today I Needed:

Today I Laughed At:

I Gave Myself Permission To:

Today I:

THE CONQUEROR BLUEPRINT

Date: I Feel:

Today Has Been: The Best Thing I've Heard Today:

My Body Feels: Today I Asked God:

I Looked At Myself In The Mirror And   I Thank God For:
Thought:

A Compliment To Myself: Today I Nurtured Myself By:

Today I Needed: Today I Laughed At:

I Gave Myself Permission To: Today I:

THE CONQUEROR BLUEPRINT

Date: I Feel:

Today Has Been: The Best Thing I've Heard Today:

My Body Feels: Today I Asked God:

I Looked At Myself In The Mirror And   I Thank God For:
Thought:

A Compliment To Myself: Today I Nurtured Myself By:

Today I Needed: Today I Laughed At:

I Gave Myself Permission To: Today I:

I Have The Right Mindset. I Have A Positive Mindset.

EVERYTHING HAS BEEN PUT INTO PERSPECTIVE.

15 WAYS LIFE HAS CHANGED SINCE DIAGNOSIS....

THE CONQUEROR BLUEPRINT

Date: I Feel:

Today Has Been: The Best Thing I've Heard Today:

My Body Feels: Today I Asked God:

I Looked At Myself In The Mirror And   I Thank God For:
Thought:

A Compliment To Myself: Today I Nurtured Myself By:

Today I Needed: Today I Laughed At:

I Gave Myself Permission To: Today I:

THE CONQUEROR BLUEPRINT

Date: I Feel:

Today Has Been: The Best Thing I've Heard Today:

My Body Feels: Today I Asked God:

I Looked At Myself In The Mirror And   I Thank God For:
Thought:

A Compliment To Myself: Today I Nurtured Myself By:

Today I Needed: Today I Laughed At:

I Gave Myself Permission To: Today I:

It's A Good Day To Kick This Cancer In The Butt.

THE CONQUEROR BLUEPRINT

Date: I Feel:

Today Has Been: The Best Thing I've Heard Today:

My Body Feels: Today I Asked God:

I Looked At Myself In The Mirror And   I Thank God For:
Thought:

A Compliment To Myself: Today I Nurtured Myself By:

Today I Needed: Today I Laughed At:

I Gave Myself Permission To: Today I:

MY PERSONAL THOUGHTS

IT'S OKAY TO FEEL HOW I FEEL RIGHT NOW.

THE CONQUEROR BLUEPRINT

Date:

I Feel:

Today Has Been:

The Best Thing I've Heard Today:

My Body Feels:

Today I Asked God:

I Looked At Myself In The Mirror And Thought:

I Thank God For:

A Compliment To Myself:

Today I Nurtured Myself By:

Today I Needed:

Today I Laughed At:

I Gave Myself Permission To:

Today I:

My Mind Is Strong Enough To Help Me Beat My Affliction.

THE CONQUEROR BLUEPRINT

Date: I Feel:

Today Has Been: The Best Thing I've Heard Today:

My Body Feels: Today I Asked God:

I Looked At Myself In The Mirror And   I Thank God For:
Thought:

A Compliment To Myself: Today I Nurtured Myself By:

Today I Needed: Today I Laughed At:

I Gave Myself Permission To: Today I:

THE CONQUEROR BLUEPRINT

Date:

I Feel:

Today Has Been:

The Best Thing I've Heard Today:

My Body Feels:

Today I Asked God:

I Looked At Myself In The Mirror And Thought:

I Thank God For:

A Compliment To Myself:

Today I Nurtured Myself By:

Today I Needed:

Today I Laughed At:

I Gave Myself Permission To:

Today I:

My Body And I Are A Team Working Together In Harmony.

A WIN FOR ME IS A WIN FOR EVERYONE.

IT'S ONE THING TO FIGHT THE FIGHT WITH OTHERS, BUT IT'S ANOTHER THING TO FIGHT THE FIGHT AND WIN ALONE.

THE CONQUEROR BLUEPRINT

Date:

I Feel:

Today Has Been:

The Best Thing I've Heard Today:

My Body Feels:

Today I Asked God:

I Looked At Myself In The Mirror And Thought:

I Thank God For:

A Compliment To Myself:

Today I Nurtured Myself By:

Today I Needed:

Today I Laughed At:

I Gave Myself Permission To:

Today I:

THE CONQUEROR BLUEPRINT

Date:

I Feel:

Today Has Been:

The Best Thing I've Heard Today:

My Body Feels:

Today I Asked God:

I Looked At Myself In The Mirror And Thought:

I Thank God For:

A Compliment To Myself:

Today I Nurtured Myself By:

Today I Needed:

Today I Laughed At:

I Gave Myself Permission To:

Today I:

Cancer Is A Lemon That I Can Squeeze To Make Lemonade.

THE CONQUEROR BLUEPRINT

Date: I Feel:

Today Has Been: The Best Thing I've Heard Today:

My Body Feels: Today I Asked God:

I Looked At Myself In The Mirror And   I Thank God For:
Thought:

A Compliment To Myself: Today I Nurtured Myself By:

Today I Needed: Today I Laughed At:

I Gave Myself Permission To: Today I:

A LETTER TO MY HEALED SELF....

THE CONQUEROR BLUEPRINT

I Am Focusing On Progress.

Date:

I Feel:

Today Has Been:

The Best Thing I've Heard Today:

My Body Feels:

Today I Asked God:

I Looked At Myself In The Mirror And Thought:

I Thank God For:

A Compliment To Myself:

Today I Nurtured Myself By:

Today I Needed:

Today I Laughed At:

I Gave Myself Permission To:

Today I:

THE CONQUEROR BLUEPRINT

Date:

I Feel:

Today Has Been:

The Best Thing I've Heard Today:

My Body Feels:

Today I Asked God:

I Looked At Myself In The Mirror And Thought:

I Thank God For:

A Compliment To Myself:

Today I Nurtured Myself By:

Today I Needed:

Today I Laughed At:

I Gave Myself Permission To:

Today I:

I'm A Sister, A Daughter, A Friend, And A Survivor.

EVEN ON MY WORST DAY, I KNOW THERE ARE BETTER DAYS TO COME.

I FIGHT FOR WHAT I LOVE. I LOVE ME SO I AM FIGHTING FOR ME.

THE CONQUEROR BLUEPRINT

Date: I Feel:

Today Has Been: The Best Thing I've Heard Today:

My Body Feels: Today I Asked God:

I Looked At Myself In The Mirror And   I Thank God For:
Thought:

A Compliment To Myself: Today I Nurtured Myself By:

Today I Needed: Today I Laughed At:

I Gave Myself Permission To: Today I:

THE CONQUEROR BLUEPRINT

Date: I Feel:

Today Has Been: The Best Thing I've Heard Today:

My Body Feels: Today I Asked God:

I Looked At Myself In The Mirror And   I Thank God For:
Thought:

A Compliment To Myself: Today I Nurtured Myself By:

Today I Needed: Today I Laughed At:

I Gave Myself Permission To: Today I:

THE CONQUEROR BLUEPRINT

Date: I Feel:

Today Has Been: The Best Thing I've Heard Today:

My Body Feels: Today I Asked God:

I Looked At Myself In The Mirror And Thought: I Thank God For:

A Compliment To Myself: Today I Nurtured Myself By:

Today I Needed: Today I Laughed At:

I Gave Myself Permission To: Today I:

I CALL THIS CHAPTER OF MY LIFE....

SOME DAYS MY OWN STRENGTH SURPRISES ME.

THE CONQUEROR BLUEPRINT

Date: I Feel:

Today Has Been: The Best Thing I've Heard Today:

My Body Feels: Today I Asked God:

I Looked At Myself In The Mirror And Thought: I Thank God For:

A Compliment To Myself: Today I Nurtured Myself By:

Today I Needed: Today I Laughed At:

I Gave Myself Permission To: Today I:

Thank You For The Life That I Shall Spend Encouraging Others.

THE CONQUEROR BLUEPRINT

Date: I Feel:

Today Has Been: The Best Thing I've Heard Today:

My Body Feels: Today I Asked God:

I Looked At Myself In The Mirror And   I Thank God For:
Thought:

A Compliment To Myself: Today I Nurtured Myself By:

Today I Needed: Today I Laughed At:

I Gave Myself Permission To: Today I:

A LETTER TO A LOVE ONE WHO HAS OR MAY EXPERIENCE THIS IN THE FUTURE....

THE CONQUEROR BLUEPRINT

Date: I Feel:

Today Has Been: The Best Thing I've Heard Today:

My Body Feels: Today I Asked God:

I Looked At Myself In The Mirror And   I Thank God For:
Thought:

A Compliment To Myself: Today I Nurtured Myself By:

Today I Needed: Today I Laughed At:

I Gave Myself Permission To: Today I:

THE CONQUEROR BLUEPRINT

Date:

I Feel:

Today Has Been:

The Best Thing I've Heard Today:

My Body Feels:

Today I Asked God:

I Looked At Myself In The Mirror And Thought:

I Thank God For:

A Compliment To Myself:

Today I Nurtured Myself By:

Today I Needed:

Today I Laughed At:

I Gave Myself Permission To:

Today I:

MY PERSONAL THOUGHTS

I REFUSE TO SURROUND MYSELF WITH ANYTHING AND ANYONE THAT DOESN'T MAKE ME HAPPY.

THE CONQUEROR BLUEPRINT

Date: I Feel:

Today Has Been: The Best Thing I've Heard Today:

My Body Feels: Today I Asked God:

I Looked At Myself In The Mirror And   I Thank God For:
Thought:

A Compliment To Myself: Today I Nurtured Myself By:

Today I Needed: Today I Laughed At:

I Gave Myself Permission To: Today I:

THE CONQUEROR BLUEPRINT

Date: I Feel:

Today Has Been: The Best Thing I've Heard Today:

My Body Feels: Today I Asked God:

I Looked At Myself In The Mirror And Thought: I Thank God For:

A Compliment To Myself: Today I Nurtured Myself By:

Today I Needed: Today I Laughed At:

I Gave Myself Permission To: Today I:

I Am Reclaiming My Life. I Am Loving Every Part Of It.

MY PERSONAL THOUGHTS

THE CONQUEROR BLUEPRINT

Date:

Today Has Been:

My Body Feels:

I Looked At Myself In The Mirror And Thought:

A Compliment To Myself:

Today I Needed:

I Gave Myself Permission To:

I Feel:

The Best Thing I've Heard Today:

Today I Asked God:

I Thank God For:

Today I Nurtured Myself By:

Today I Laughed At:

Today I:

I Am A Friend To My Body. I Forgive My Body And Treat It With Love.

THIS TIME OF MY LIFE IS MAKING ME REALIZE THAT BY FIGHTING, I AM FIGHTING FOR A SECOND CHANCE TO LIVE MY LIFE ON MY TERMS.

IN THIS CHAPTER OF MY LIFE, ALL I NEED IS LOVE.

THE CONQUEROR BLUEPRINT

Date: I Feel:

Today Has Been: The Best Thing I've Heard Today:

My Body Feels: Today I Asked God:

I Looked At Myself In The Mirror And   I Thank God For:
Thought:

A Compliment To Myself: Today I Nurtured Myself By:

Today I Needed: Today I Laughed At:

I Gave Myself Permission To: Today I:

THE CONQUEROR BLUEPRINT

Date:

Today Has Been:

My Body Feels:

I Looked At Myself In The Mirror And Thought:

A Compliment To Myself:

Today I Needed:

I Gave Myself Permission To:

I Feel:

The Best Thing I've Heard Today:

Today I Asked God:

I Thank God For:

Today I Nurtured Myself By:

Today I Laughed At:

Today I:

I Am Experiencing The Miracle Of Physical And Spiritual Healing.

THE CONQUEROR BLUEPRINT

Date: I Feel:

Today Has Been: The Best Thing I've Heard Today:

My Body Feels: Today I Asked God:

I Looked At Myself In The Mirror And   I Thank God For:
Thought:

A Compliment To Myself: Today I Nurtured Myself By:

Today I Needed: Today I Laughed At:

I Gave Myself Permission To: Today I:

THE CONQUEROR BLUEPRINT

Date: I Feel:

Today Has Been: The Best Thing I've Heard Today:

My Body Feels: Today I Asked God:

I Looked At Myself In The Mirror And   I Thank God For:
Thought:

A Compliment To Myself: Today I Nurtured Myself By:

Today I Needed: Today I Laughed At:

I Gave Myself Permission To: Today I:

A LETTER TO GOD....

MY GOD IS FIGHTING MY BATTLES FOR ME. I TRUST IN HIM.

MY PERSONAL THOUGHTS

THE CONQUEROR BLUEPRINT

Date:

Today Has Been:

My Body Feels:

I Looked At Myself In The Mirror And Thought:

A Compliment To Myself:

Today I Needed:

I Gave Myself Permission To:

I Feel:

The Best Thing I've Heard Today:

Today I Asked God:

I Thank God For:

Today I Nurtured Myself By:

Today I Laughed At:

Today I:

Peace Flows Through My Body, Mind And Spirit.

THE CONQUEROR BLUEPRINT

Date: I Feel:

Today Has Been: The Best Thing I've Heard Today:

My Body Feels: Today I Asked God:

I Looked At Myself In The Mirror And   I Thank God For:
Thought:

A Compliment To Myself: Today I Nurtured Myself By:

Today I Needed: Today I Laughed At:

I Gave Myself Permission To: Today I:

THE CONQUEROR BLUEPRINT

Date:

Today Has Been:

My Body Feels:

I Looked At Myself In The Mirror And Thought:

A Compliment To Myself:

Today I Needed:

I Gave Myself Permission To:

I Feel:

The Best Thing I've Heard Today:

Today I Asked God:

I Thank God For:

Today I Nurtured Myself By:

Today I Laughed At:

Today I:

I'm Visualizing Good Times And I'm Grateful For My Friends' Support.

THE CONQUEROR BLUEPRINT

Date: I Feel:

Today Has Been: The Best Thing I've Heard Today:

My Body Feels: Today I Asked God:

I Looked At Myself In The Mirror And   I Thank God For:
Thought:

A Compliment To Myself: Today I Nurtured Myself By:

Today I Needed: Today I Laughed At:

I Gave Myself Permission To: Today I:

THE CONQUEROR BLUEPRINT

Date: I Feel:

Today Has Been: The Best Thing I've Heard Today:

My Body Feels: Today I Asked God:

I Looked At Myself In The Mirror And   I Thank God For:
Thought:

A Compliment To Myself: Today I Nurtured Myself By:

Today I Needed: Today I Laughed At:

I Gave Myself Permission To: Today I:

I Am Filled With Vitality, Energy And Physical Stamina.

I REFUSED TO BE REDUCED AND DEFINED BY WHAT HAS HAPPENED TO ME. I WILL BE RECOGNIZED BY HOW I HANDLE IT.

THE CONQUEROR BLUEPRINT

Date:

I Feel:

Today Has Been:

The Best Thing I've Heard Today:

My Body Feels:

Today I Asked God:

I Looked At Myself In The Mirror And Thought:

I Thank God For:

A Compliment To Myself:

Today I Nurtured Myself By:

Today I Needed:

Today I Laughed At:

I Gave Myself Permission To:

Today I:

I Think, Speak, And Act Nothing But In Perfect Health.

THE CONQUEROR BLUEPRINT

I Claim The Healing Power That Expresses Itself In Me In All Ways.

Date:

Today Has Been:

My Body Feels:

I Looked At Myself In The Mirror And Thought:

A Compliment To Myself:

Today I Needed:

I Gave Myself Permission To:

I Feel:

The Best Thing I've Heard Today:

Today I Asked God:

I Thank God For:

Today I Nurtured Myself By:

Today I Laughed At:

Today I:

THE CONQUEROR BLUEPRINT

Date: | I Feel:

Today Has Been: | The Best Thing I've Heard Today:

My Body Feels: | Today I Asked God:

I Looked At Myself In The Mirror And Thought: | I Thank God For:

A Compliment To Myself: | Today I Nurtured Myself By:

Today I Needed: | Today I Laughed At:

I Gave Myself Permission To: | Today I:

THE CONQUEROR BLUEPRINT

Date: I Feel:

Today Has Been: The Best Thing I've Heard Today:

My Body Feels: Today I Asked God:

I Looked At Myself In The Mirror And   I Thank God For:
Thought:

A Compliment To Myself: Today I Nurtured Myself By:

Today I Needed: Today I Laughed At:

I Gave Myself Permission To: Today I:

GREAT THINGS ABOUT MY LIFE....

I AM PROUD OF MYSELF.

THE CONQUEROR BLUEPRINT

Date: I Feel:

Today Has Been: The Best Thing I've Heard Today:

My Body Feels: Today I Asked God:

I Looked At Myself In The Mirror And   I Thank God For:
Thought:

A Compliment To Myself: Today I Nurtured Myself By:

Today I Needed: Today I Laughed At:

I Gave Myself Permission To: Today I:

THE CONQUEROR BLUEPRINT

Date: I Feel:

Today Has Been: The Best Thing I've Heard Today:

My Body Feels: Today I Asked God:

I Looked At Myself In The Mirror And   I Thank God For:
Thought:

A Compliment To Myself: Today I Nurtured Myself By:

Today I Needed: Today I Laughed At:

I Gave Myself Permission To: Today I:

THE CONQUEROR BLUEPRINT

Date:

I Feel:

Today Has Been:

The Best Thing I've Heard Today:

My Body Feels:

Today I Asked God:

I Looked At Myself In The Mirror And Thought:

I Thank God For:

A Compliment To Myself:

Today I Nurtured Myself By:

Today I Needed:

Today I Laughed At:

I Gave Myself Permission To:

Today I:

I Honor My Body And All Of Its Needs.

DEAR BREAST, YOU ARE BEAUTIFUL.

MY BODY IS AMAZING.

THE CONQUEROR BLUEPRINT

Date:

I Feel:

Today Has Been:

The Best Thing I've Heard Today:

My Body Feels:

Today I Asked God:

I Looked At Myself In The Mirror And Thought:

I Thank God For:

A Compliment To Myself:

Today I Nurtured Myself By:

Today I Needed:

Today I Laughed At:

I Gave Myself Permission To:

Today I:

THE CONQUEROR BLUEPRINT

Date:

I Feel:

Today Has Been:

The Best Thing I've Heard Today:

My Body Feels:

Today I Asked God:

I Looked At Myself In The Mirror And Thought:

I Thank God For:

A Compliment To Myself:

Today I Nurtured Myself By:

Today I Needed:

Today I Laughed At:

I Gave Myself Permission To:

Today I:

My Positive Energy Heals My Body And Keeps Me Healthy.

THE CONQUEROR BLUEPRINT

Date:

I Feel:

Today Has Been:

The Best Thing I've Heard Today:

My Body Feels:

Today I Asked God:

I Looked At Myself In The Mirror And Thought:

I Thank God For:

A Compliment To Myself:

Today I Nurtured Myself By:

Today I Needed:

Today I Laughed At:

I Gave Myself Permission To:

Today I:

I'm Feeling Better Already As I'm With The People Who Matter.

MY SPIRIT FEELS....

MY PERSONAL THOUGHTS

THE CONQUEROR BLUEPRINT

Date: I Feel:

Today Has Been: The Best Thing I've Heard Today:

My Body Feels: Today I Asked God:

I Looked At Myself In The Mirror And   I Thank God For:
Thought:

A Compliment To Myself: Today I Nurtured Myself By:

Today I Needed: Today I Laughed At:

I Gave Myself Permission To: Today I:

I Am So Thankful For Every Moment I Have In My Body.

THE CONQUEROR BLUEPRINT

Date: I Feel:

Today Has Been: The Best Thing I've Heard Today:

My Body Feels: Today I Asked God:

I Looked At Myself In The Mirror And   I Thank God For:
Thought:

A Compliment To Myself: Today I Nurtured Myself By:

Today I Needed: Today I Laughed At:

I Gave Myself Permission To: Today I:

I NO LONGER TAKE FOR GRANTED....

THE CONQUEROR BLUEPRINT

Date: I Feel:

Today Has Been: The Best Thing I've Heard Today:

My Body Feels: Today I Asked God:

I Looked At Myself In The Mirror And   I Thank God For:
Thought:

A Compliment To Myself: Today I Nurtured Myself By:

Today I Needed: Today I Laughed At:

I Gave Myself Permission To: Today I:

THE CONQUEROR BLUEPRINT

Date:

I Feel:

Today Has Been:

The Best Thing I've Heard Today:

My Body Feels:

Today I Asked God:

I Looked At Myself In The Mirror And Thought:

I Thank God For:

A Compliment To Myself:

Today I Nurtured Myself By:

Today I Needed:

Today I Laughed At:

I Gave Myself Permission To:

Today I:

I Am Thankful For The Challenges In My Life.

MY PERSONAL THOUGHTS

I MAKE MYSELF FEEL GOOD.